Bumpers

The Framework for Finding Your Personal Abundance, Maximum Productivity, Greatest Profits and Highest Quality of Life

NIC PETERSON

Copyright © 2023 by Nic Peterson. All rights reserved.

No part of this book may be reproduced in any form or by any electronic or mechanical means, including information storage and retrieval systems, without written permission from the author, except for the use of brief quotations in a book review.

ISBN: 978-1-956955-34-7 (paperback)

978-1-956955-35-4 (ebook)

Praise for Bumpers and Nic Peterson

"*Bumpers* is a short but profound and extremely useful book. What Nic Peterson writes on page four makes it worth the entire price of the book. Go read it now."

—Joe Polish, Founder of Genius Network

"Every once in a while, someone shows up in my life that I describe to my wife as having a 'bent frame.' They're tweaked. The mental math they use to manifest possibility and solve dilemmas is different. Unorthodox methods and unshakeable certainty about what can be achieved are their trademarks. What they touch turns to gold. Nic Peterson has a 'bent frame.' And that makes *Bumpers* a key read for anyone who wants to make extraordinary their normal. It is an inspiring work that shows people the fundamental actions that can enable their exponential productivity and, better yet, have fun doing it. I finished *Bumpers* in one short sitting. I can't recommend it highly enough."

—Dr. Jeff Spencer, nine-year Tour de France chiropractor and mindset coach and winner of 45 Olympic, world, Tour de France and national championships as well as nine Olympic gold medals

“Selfless, go-giving, ambitious, smart and loving are just a few words for Nic. In business and in life, Nic is one of the best men I know. He has stood with me through my successes and near death. I can’t speak highly enough of Nic. If you have the opportunity to work with him, learn from him or be his friend, I say go all in—because he certainly will!”

—John Rowley, bestselling author, Clickbank board member and fitness and lifestyle master

“Nic is one of the most uniquely skilled and brilliant people I’ve ever met. He operates with integrity and is an amazing leader that has a unique ability to build strategic relationships. What stands out the most to me about Nic is that while nearly everyone is trying to complicate things and hide behind complex unproven or non-duplicatable strategies, he keeps things simple and uses common sense to hone in on the fastest, most direct path to achieving your goals while trying to strategically avoid friction and stress. In order words, he’s a master at multiplication by subtraction. We need more people like Nic in the world.”

—Timothy Dick, Founder/CEO of VOIPO and ProfitLayer.com

"Nic understands how to play the long game. Work with him if you want to consistently win; don't if you just want a quick win before burning out."

—Dan Nicholson, Founder of Nth Degree CPAs

Contents

Foreword

It is impossible to overlook the extent to which we are impacted by the extraordinary people and relationships that come into our lives, especially when one of those relationships is with someone like Nic Peterson.

In February of 2018, I was introduced via email to Nic by a mutual friend, Dan Giuglianotti. Dan is Nic's partner in Mastery Mode, and he thought the two of us could really connect and potentially make beautiful music together...and he was right.

Our first conversation lasted for over two-and-a-half hours—the time it took for me to drive from Brea in Orange Country, California to Ventura. It felt like maybe 15 minutes; time stood still.

Nearly three years since that encounter, I am proud to call Nic not only one of my dearest friends but also a business partner, confidant, advisor and even house guest.

Bumpers could have easily been called *How to*

Win Bigger and Longer by Doing What You Are Already Doing Every Day, but that would exceed Nic's economy of words. Nic has an amazing way of saying little but revealing volumes of meaning and purpose. The length of *Bumpers* is an example of his ability to deliver massive, life-changing impact in bite-sized doses.

I am one of the very few people on earth that has the privilege of watching the mind of this man evolve in real time...and it is a thing to watch. His ability to compile reams of data, analyze it for the useful parts and then come up with a unique strategy for a client (or partner and friend) so it can be naturally, effectively, efficiently and sustainably executed is a wonderful combination of experience, science and art that is so "right on" for the person he is advising that the individual feels like it has been there all along... because it has.

The biggest challenge people have is how to share Nic with others. They just know that they have a conversation with him, and now their life has been forever altered—that they have the sort of clarity and certainty that can turn a seven-year goal into a two-year goal or a six-figure launch into a seven-figure launch without really having to make any massive changes to their initial plan.

I have seen it. I am known for being a fairly effective coach/consultant/advisor with a proclivity for compelling messaging, and even I was having a hard time explaining the magic of Nic to people without sounding clichéd or like I was generalizing. But, after

Day 7 of Nicsmas 2020 (Nicsmas2020.com), it finally hit me in a way that will not only forever change the way I see and introduce Nic to others, but also change the way Nic sees himself.

This is what I wrote to him that day:

> *You are not a coach, a consultant or a teacher . . . you are a sculptor, carving away at the noise and complexity of what we think we are supposed to do based on all the advice, posts, ads and offers out there, finally delivering a beautiful piece of art uniquely carved to reveal our most fulfilled, happy and prosperous life . . . the best version of our individual selves and the role we play in our own happiness and in the service of others.*

This would just about explain it, but Nic is always evolving, so the very best way to begin to understand and benefit from his "sculpting" is to start with the very foundation: his Operating System. *Bumpers* is that OS.

In short, visual and meaningful language, *Bumpers* is going to introduce you to the most important person you will ever meet in your life: YOU.

For many people that have been on that search for the next new thing that will seemingly change the game, this book may be a little painful to read. But it will also be enormously liberating.

There are exercises in this book that might be a

bit excruciating to the more learned of readers, but until you complete them with purpose and intention, they will haunt you—and the only way you will be able to cast out the ghost will be to commit to YOU by pursuing the best version of the life you live.

Bumpers is the key to unlocking a system that provides a way of being that will provide you a life of happiness, prosperity and fulfillment on your terms for the rest of your life.

A system that has been there all along, waiting for you to find it, hidden in plain sight.

I look forward to taking this journey with you.

Fondly,
—Jeff Moore
Director, Global Protein Group
Partner, The Network as Mastery Mode
Founder, Thursday Night Boardroom

Introduction

"Most prefer the certainty of misery to
the misery of uncertainty."
—Virginia Satir

THE DEVIL YOU KNOW

Imagine you're in a miserable relationship.

Now imagine that there are two doors before you. Behind door number one is a five percent chance of being happier. Behind door number two is the life you already know.

Your choices are between a five percent chance of being happier or a zero percent chance of being happier. Which do you choose?

In theory, door one is the obvious answer. In reality, most people will choose door two because we prefer what is familiar, *even if it's they know it's harmful to us*. The misery we know now is less frightening than the uncertainty of the unknown.

We see this when our friends stay in bad relationships or horrible jobs. The fact that many of our friends are still our friends is proof that we hold onto what we know, even if it doesn't serve us.

It's true even in our daily interactions. Next time someone asks you what you do, tell them something they can't easily understand and watch them squirm.

My favorite description of what I do is either:

"I help smart people get out of their own way."

Or:

"I collect smart people by making them a lot of money."

These are my favorite responses because the reaction to them tells me a lot about the other party.

I would guess that about 96 percent of people try to exit the conversation as soon as possible. *The misery of uncertainty.* They don't even want to have conversation with someone they can't quickly make sense of. The other four percent, open-minded and driven by curiosity, want to know more. I do this because it's more important to me to quickly identify that four percent than it is for someone else to know what I do. That four percent makes for the most interesting conversation, anyway. They are curiosity-driven, they are open to the unknown, and they all end up asking the same question: a version of, *"How do you do so many things in so many industries?"*

The answer is I've discovered a way to...

LEARN STUFF AND GET PAID A LOT TO DO IT

How?

By helping smart people get out of their own way. The book in front of you is my attempt at explaining my method for getting smart people out of their own way. Since you've made it this far, I am assuming you're open to new ways of thinking and behaving.

Note: The original draft said "open to starting something new." It's more important to me that you stop doing the things that are hurting you than it is to get you to start doing new things.

I am grateful that you are taking the time to read *Bumpers*. What I hope is that you also take the time to start the exercises in the pages below. *The brain has a proclivity for finishing what it has started.* Getting started is the most difficult part, and you've already done that.

Bumpers is a good example. It was never supposed to be a book. I woke up at 3 am on a Saturday, drove to the office and started writing. At 2:45 that morning, I was lying in bed trying to fall asleep when I realized everyone I had worked with had been asking the same question:

"Am I ever going to be happy?"

Dozens of industries, hundreds of different business models, personalities and personal preferences. But the same question. Once it hit me, I knew I was not going to be able to get back to sleep. So I rolled out of bed, admired my dogs, who were curled up like little cinnamon rolls, and drove to my office to write. I thought I would write a few sentences, get distracted and be able to go back to sleep. *But the brain has a proclivity for finishing what it has started.* After four hours of brain-dumping, I felt like I had finished.

Once "finished," I shared it with a close friend, Tim. Tim and I used to host private client events in our Lake Forest office in California, and at our next private client event, Tim printed off copies and handed them out to everyone. There were about 30 world-class entrepreneurs in that room getting a copy of a rough, unedited brain dump. I remember feeling uncomfortable as it was being handed out, so I hedged a little by warning them it was a rough draft and would be finished later. In the following days, I received dozens of requests to leave it as was, typos and all.

If you are one of those 30 people and you are reading this now: thank you. *Bumpers* would have died on Tim's desk without your feedback and support. I've updated some of the language and added some models, but little has changed from the original.

Important Note:

Bumpers is not designed to be a "shelf-help" book. It's too tiny to look good on your bookshelf, anyway. It's not designed to teach or tell you anything you don't already know. My hope is that you carry it with you and use it as a tool to help you put what you know into action. If you are reading this now, you are smart enough to get the things you want in life. *Bumpers* exists to help turn common sense into common practice and to identify when common sense is not going to serve you.

I am often accused of having many overnight successes. Most days, I get to do whatever I want to do. I am convinced you can, too. It's not a matter of acquiring more information or "knowing" more stuff. Stacking abstract theory on top of abstract theory can be crippling. It interferes with the most important thing: *consistently applying what is useful to you.*

There is an excellent chance that you are more talented than I am. It's not a high bar. Most people I work with are more intelligent and have more technical knowledge than I do. Information is not in short supply; it's everywhere and it's free. What is scarce is the practical application, the frameworks for what to do with all this information and a system to do it consistently. More importantly, frameworks to apply the information in a way that is going to make *you* happy.

That's what this book is about. I am not going to tell you what should make you happy, I'm just going to share what I have learned about attaining it once you figure out what it is.

It starts with The Gaps.

THE GAPS

Marketing is about creating desire.

Desire is a function of realizing there is a gap between where you are now and where you want to be. Desire is good when it fuels us to change our behavior to close that gap. Well-intentioned marketers, educators and self-help gurus often widen the gap; they create more desire to motivate you to take action. In an attempt to sell you on change, they introduce more things you should be doing or more things you didn't even know you needed. If you take in new information about what you should be doing at a rate that is faster than you are modifying your behavior, the gap is growing.

Often, the gap between where you are now and where you have been convinced you should be becomes so wide that anxiety replaces desire.

This is the first and most obvious gap: the gap between the "you are here" sticker on the map and where you want to be. This is the first gap we must address. Without the "you are here" sticker, nothing else will work.

In my experience, people have a vague idea of where they want to go and no clue about their current location. I've heard many explanations about what prevents us from getting clarity on these two locations. Here are the two that most closely match my observations:

1. Fear Of Defining Success

Often, high-achieving people avoid defining success because defining success also defines failure. For example, let's pretend that "success" is having dinner with your kids every night while they are still young. Once that's defined, you have to face the feeling of failure every time you miss dinner with your kids. By defining what success is, you can no longer hide behind the other trappings of success. The more specific your definition of success, the more difficult it becomes to hide behind the things that are not.

As long as you haven't defined it for yourself, you can hide behind Stripe screenshots, Ferraris and Instagram Reels.

The Harvard Business Review has a great piece called "Teaching Smart People How To Learn." It demonstrates how smart people actively avoid learning to maintain and hide behind the label of "being smart." Learning something requires admission of not already knowing it and that admission threatens the identity of being smart. Instead of learning, smart people are quick to show off what they already know in hopes that enough of their points will be valid, impress others and allow them to keep their identity.

Getting what you want in life is often hindered by hiding behind the label of "successful." The things we actually want in life are often complex, making them difficult to quantify and achieve. Clearly defining those things threatens our identity as "successful." The more specificity, the higher the perceived threat to the identity. Instead of going for what they want in life, successful people are quick to show off all the things they already have in hopes of protecting their identity.

To protect the identity of "successful," the brain fights hard to maintain ambiguity in a personal definition of success.

2. Fighting To Maintain The Delusion

Few people are willing to be honest about who and what they are or *who and what they are not.* Many life transformations start with physical fitness because it forces reality upon you. It's easy to accept that your hamstrings are tight or that you're out of breath. It's much more difficult to accept the reality of your other insecurities. Fitness often provides the first crack in the armor of self-delusion. Getting an accurate "you are here" sticker requires chipping away at the rest of that delusion.

The brain works overtime to protect the delusion about what we are or are not. It will convince us that every mirror we look into is a window; that the problems are somewhere "out there" instead of somewhere "in here." It's tough to get a hold on reality when every mirror looks like a window to you.

To protect the delusion of self, the brain fights

hard to convince you that everything wrong with the world is "out there." This makes an accurate starting position impossible to pinpoint.

After identifying the gap between where you are and where you want to be, the next gap to look for is a concept I picked up from my friend Dr. Trevor Kashey:

THE INTENTION-INTERVENTION GAP

I met Trevor in 2012.

All I knew about him is that he was working on his Ph.D. and everyone he worked with was getting super jacked. So I asked him to help me with my nutrition. He agreed, as long as I followed instructions.

This dude is a biochemist, so I expected an elaborate plan with lots of...science. This is how our conversation went:

Trevor: "So you're outside 8-10 hours a day in Florida?"

Nic: "Yes."

T: "Okay, drink one gallon of water a day next week."

N: "And then what?"

T: "Let me know when you drink a gallon of water a day for an entire week."

A week later I messaged him:

N: "Okay, now what?"

T: "Did you drink a gallon of water every day this week?"

N: "Yeah. I mean, five of the days I finished the

whole gallon. The other two I just wasn't paying attention and fell short."

T: "Let me know when you drink a gallon of water a day for an entire week. Until then, don't ask me again."

But where is all the fancy science stuff? I remember thinking to myself. About a week a later, I started to understand his point.

His point was that five out of seven is 71.4 percent. I was doing what I planned on doing 71 percent of the time. Would you drive a car that only started 71 percent of the time you tried to start it? Or buy a computer that only turned on 71.4 percent of the time you expected it to turn on?

I wouldn't.

That is a huge gap between the expectation and reality and the outcomes would be unreliable. Will I get my homework done? Depends on if my computer cooperates today. Will I get to school to turn it in? Maybe, my car only starts 74 percent of the time.

The fanciest science stuff in the world isn't going to make a difference if I can't hold up my end of the bargain more than 71 percent of the time.

What Trevor did was help me realize that if I'm only following 71 percent of the plan, I should have no expectations. Further, it pointed out that I thought five days out of seven was good. *I thought I was following the plan.* What Trevor knew is that I would gauge the efficacy of his advice based on my results. Then, I would incorrectly attribute the results to that advice. It would be bad for him and bad for me; I wouldn't actually be learning anything. I'd have just kept changing plans, blaming the plans and keeping my behavior about the same.

He helped me see the intention-intervention gap:

Intention: *What you intend or plan on doing with your knowledge.*

Intervention: *Your actual behavior.*

Gap: *The discrepancy between the two.*

The intention-intervention gap is the gap between:

- What you say you are going to do and what you actually do.
- What you say you want and what your behavior suggests you want.
- Your action plan and your implementation.

Dan Nicholson tackles this topic in his bestselling book *Rigging The Game*. What he refers to as the gap between "espoused values" and "values in action" results in a "tug of war" against yourself. A war of attrition where even if you win, you lose. The biggest victims of this civil war? Smart people, like you.

Most coaches, consultants and self-help programs focus on the intention or the "espoused values." They tell you more of the things you *should* be doing, without regard to whether it's widening or closing the gap for you. "Do this if you want to get to where you want to be" presents the illusion of helping you close one gap. But if your behavior doesn't change to match the set of directions, it hasn't done anything at all for you. In fact, it's probably widened the gap.

For example:

If we plan on exercising five days a week and only make it to the gym four times, there is a gap. If someone tells us we should exercise six days a week with no proof of actually being able to do five, they are widening the gap.

If we recite "The Good Samaritan" well and then treat strangers poorly, there is a gap.

The crippling anxiety many people feel is not a byproduct of a strategy or a plan, nor are feelings of powerlessness a byproduct of our behavior alone. They are both byproducts of *the dissonance created by the gap between the two*. The narrower the gap, the less anxiety we have about closing it. The closer the behavior matches the plan, the more reality meets our expectations. The more often reality meets expectations, the tighter the feedback loop. The tighter the feedback loop, the more power we have over the outcome.

The goal of *Bumpers* is to identify and then systematically close these gaps. To do that, *we need to fight our human desire to know more than we do until we are doing what we know.*

INTELLECTUAL COLORBLINDNESS

Across the top of my website is a header that says:

~~Guru. Expert~~. Student.

My goal there is to imply that I am a student first.

For the sake of clarity and completeness, I'll explain what I mean. When I say I am a student, I mean I am always trying to learn in order to increase my intelligence. My working definitions for the above are as follows:

Intelligence:

The ability to get what you want.

(Credit to Dr. Todd Snyder for this practical definition of a difficult-to-quantify word.)

Learning:

Modifying behavior based on new information.

Student:

A person who increases their ability to get what they want by changing their behavior based on new information.

You do not have to adopt or agree with these definitions. I am just making mine explicit. I want working definitions that are practical, applicable and that convert theory to action.

In his *Incerto* series, author Nassim Nicholas Taleb addresses theories vs. actions from various angles. For example, in *Antifragile*, he shares a story about a tribe researchers believed to be colorblind. Members of the tribe were unable to verbally distinguish a blue string from a red string, so researchers concluded they couldn't see the color blue.

It was later discovered that the tribe members

could match the strings to a corresponding color swatch. They matched the red strings to the red swatch and the blue string to the blue swatch with 100 percent accuracy. Turns out they could distinguish between the two colors, but they didn't have a word for the color blue in their language.

They were linguistically, not biologically, colorblind.

They were handicapped in theory, not action—a handicap that is only limiting in an intellectual world where words matter more than actions.

It serves as a good reminder to avoid a dependence on narratives.

It is easy to mistake *intellectualizing* actions for actually *doing* actions. You don't need to understand the various theorems of aerodynamics to ride a bike; we need a name for blue in narrative, but not in application.

To paraphrase Taleb:

It is the thinker lacking the word for blue who is handicapped. The doer is not.

I worked with Trevor for many years. What I learned in that process is simple: do the damn thing first. Later, if I'm still curious, I can learn the theory behind it. Turns out that most of the time, I didn't care as much for the theory as I thought. I thought I did, because I thought knowing the theory would help me change my life for the better. I was wrong.

It's the doing, not the knowing that changes your life.

Because I'd rather experience the benefits than know more about the thing, I've made a habit of doing first and understanding later.

I'll never claim to have figured it all out, but what I been able to do is close the intention-intervention gap for myself and hundreds of others. I'm going to share how I do that with you now, but there are a few things you should know.

First, closing the gap is not destination, it's a skill. It's never "done." As long as you are living life, you are learning. As long as you are learning, the gap will widen. What you want will change and the gap will widen again. This is as much about learning the skill of minimizing the gap on an ongoing basis as it is about closing it. Think of it as "gap maintenance."

Second, you must do. There are only two ways to close the gap: *change your behavior or want nothing and do nothing.* As long as you want something you don't already have, your behavior must change. Thinking about stuff is a precursor to action, not an action itself. The more you think, read and study without action, the wider the gap becomes. The wider the gap, the greater the anxiety and the greater the risk of paralysis. You must commit to taking action more often than intellectualizing action.

Finally, I am writing this because I value our relationship. In case this is the only exchange we ever have, I want to share the most valuable thing I have to share with you. This will be more valuable to the right people than anything technical or tactical I could give you. You will learn about yourself in the following pages. I've tried to give you the framework to help create a system that helps you get what you want out of life. I hope it works for you as well as it has worked for me and many others.

If you want to start monitoring your progress right away, go to freebumpersbook.com. There is a workbook and audio companion. The audio companion is not me reading this book, it's a recorded dialogue about the application(s). It cost $100,000 to be in the room that day; now, it's yours for free.

Final Warning: If you want to learn a bunch of stuff you will never apply, close this book now. There is likely nothing in the following pages you don't already know. If you are ready to shift from being the thinker to the doer, read on.

Onward.

Chapter 1

Bumpers

"All I want to know is where I'm going to die so that I do not go there."

—Charlie Munger

Humans are incredible. Both solo endeavors and unified efforts can yield incredible, previously unimaginable things. We are also flawed. And one of our greatest flaws is:

We fail to appreciate when bad things don't happen.

Let that sink in for a moment.

Consider both the excitement and the relief of digging yourself out of a hole. Whether paying off debt, losing weight or regaining your health, these are all things we celebrate.

Now think about how it feels when a close friend

loses 50 pounds and gets off all their medication. It's exciting. You get a hit of dopamine when you hear the news. They get a hit of dopamine when you congratulate them. Everyone experiences an emotional high. These moments are worth appreciating. Like you, I want good things to happen to people I care about.

But consider this:

How much time, effort, and suffering went into digging out of that hole? That's a tremendous amount of resources spent to get back to baseline. Resources expended and time spent to get back to baseline are resources that are not used to move forward or make progress. How much progress would that person have made if instead of allocating all those resources to recovery, they allocated them to forward progress?

After doing the math, you'd think it would be easy to appreciate when bad things don't happen. But when is the last time you celebrated avoiding something negative? Have you thrown a party for your friends who never faced bankruptcy? Have you congratulated your sister for never gaining any excess weight?

Doubtful.

And I don't blame you. That would be super weird.

Not only would it be weird, *it doesn't feel rewarding*. Getting rescued feels more rewarding than avoiding danger does. Saving people looks a lot sexier than pointing out potholes for them to avoid. This creates an insidious incentive problem. You're probably aware that big pharma makes a lot more money from selling the cure than it does from selling prevention. Why?

Are they evil? Maybe. But: windows and mirrors. Let's not forgot our role in this.

It's easier to sell the cure than it is to sell the prevention *<u>because it feels better to buy it.</u>*

It was the most terrifying sound I'd ever heard.

I was finishing up a workout session with a group of friends. They gathered around the bench press as I finished my last set. All I could hear was the blaring music echoing through an otherwise empty gym. Until it happened. It sounded like my spotter had started ripping through sheets of bubble wrap in my left ear. A few pops, a rip and a suddenly numb upper body. I had torn both of my hamstrings before, but I'd never heard the sound of a muscle tearing before. Not like this.

It didn't take long for my spotters to realize something was wrong and take the weight from me. To this day, I think about how grateful I am they were paying attention. By that point, I knew I had torn something. It was my left pec. As the bruising started to show, I asked myself, *Now what?*

There are two people I trusted most with this kind of thing. One of them lived with me, and the other would always answer a call from a friend. After asking some questions, both said a version of the same thing:

"Given what I see/hear, you likely won't need surgery. The tendon is still attached."

Each gave me a plan and things to look out for. If I was not able to make progress according to plan, an MRI and/or surgery might be necessary. If I was on track with my rehab plan, it wouldn't be.

The next day, four different doctors told me I needed to get an MRI and have surgery immediately. They offered to do the MRI, make referrals to specialists and help in any way possible. They went above and beyond to get me to take action. I told one of my two trusted friends that I was thinking I should go get an MRI and surgery.

He told me he would support me either way—and then he reminded me of the danger of seeking "positive action" when non-action will get the job done.

I didn't get an MRI. I didn't get surgery. A successful surgery would have taken longer to recover from than my actual recovery time was, and that doesn't include the cost and potential complications of surgery. Through that process, I gained a new appreciation for the "prevention people."

Even with my newfound appreciation for prevention, I know that I have to continue to actively practice appreciation for non-action. It prevents me from falling into the trap of the "good feels" of positive action.

Sometimes the best action is no action.

At the time, all the specialists trying to help me do something seemed more heroic than my friends who suggested doing nothing—but they were also introducing me to something that was far riskier.

It's easy to appreciate the heroic surgeon. It's not so easy to appreciate doing nothing.

Prevention and non-action do not come with cheap, easy dopamine. Our brains' cravings for dopamine cause us to seek emotional highs. Seeking emotional highs, we overvalue rescuers and "positive action."

Imagine for a moment that you fall off a ladder hanging Christmas lights. That night, you go get two opinions from back specialists. The first tells you that you can take some aspirin and a nap and you'll be fine; if not, he will get some imaging done, but it's best to reserve judgment for a night. The second says he can put you on the operating table right now and save your back!

If you elect to get surgery and it's successful, that surgeon gets paid more than the one who told you to wait a day. He also looks like more of a hero. Once you recover from your surgery and can walk again, it feels like a miracle. You feel great, your surgeon feels great and your friends celebrate your recovery.

But what if the first dude was right and sleeping it off would have been enough? The surgeon that "did nothing" and sent you home exposed you to far less risk. And the cost to you? A couple of bucks for aspirin. The resources that went into recovery could have gone to making progress in important areas of your life.

Instead, the bias toward positive action made the

second surgeon seem more exciting, more helpful and more heroic. He got the business, he got paid and then everyone got congratulated for their part. The collective dopamine surge is far greater choosing the rescuer over the preventer.

To be clear, I am not suggesting we should not appreciate when good things happen. The firefighter that risks his life to save your child is a hero and deserves acknowledgment. But what about the guy who builds fireproof houses? Would we celebrate him the same way? And what are the long-term consequences of not doing so?

Humans are hardwired to seek attention, recognition and rewards. Dopamine is a helluva chemical. It's human nature, and human nature is not wrong. The hardwiring is not the problem. Where I see an issue is the difference between the incentives to put out fires and the incentives to prevent them. The chemical, financial and social rewards of the rescue or recovery are massive—so massive and rewarding that they can blind us to the long-term consequences.

In a state of sobriety, it's clear that prevention is the most efficient path forward. But it's not the path most traveled. There is little short-term reward on that path because there is little short-term incentive for preventing fires.

In fact, if we want a quick dopamine hit, we can start a fire real quick and then rush to put it out to get our fix. Ask any entrepreneur. Entrepreneurs hate boring stuff. To avoid it, we'll start fires all over the place so we can put them out and go home with a win. *We can end the day in the same place or worse than we started it and call it a win.* Ridiculous on one level, and very real on another.

It's also very real to someone who is celebrating their 50-pound weight loss—for the fifth time. I have empathy for yo-yo dieters because I know many of them, and their struggle is real. Their pain is real. I have had thousands of conversations with men and women who can't get off the yo-yo treadmill. The whole incentive structure makes it nearly impossible.

Let's play this out:

If this is the fifth time Sally has lost the same 50 pounds, she has done a tremendous amount of work. Losing 50 pounds five times means she put in the effort to lose 250 pounds in her lifetime. That is a ton of effort and time committed. Her brain has also logged a bunch of wins. A win for each time she hit her goal, that's five. A win for each time someone congratulated her for reaching her goal, at least another five. Depending on how many people she knows, her brain could have registered hundreds of wins.

A lot of effort toward weight loss? Check.

A lot of wins about weight loss? Check.

A lot of recognition from others? Check.

Results:

- Sally's brain is registering wins and society is reinforcing them.
- She is still in the same place she was decades ago when she started this journey.
- She put in significant effort over the years just to be in the same place or worse.

Contrast that with what would have happened had Sally never gained the weight to begin with. The efforts that went into losing weight could have gone into making incremental progress. It would never be drastic, but over the years, it would be progress.

A lot of effort toward weight loss? No. The effort

went into forward progress or was redirected to something else important.

A lot of wins about weight loss? No. The brain isn't registering maintenance as a win.

A lot of recognition from others? No. Other humans aren't celebrating Sally's maintenance.

Results:

- Sally's brain is registering fewer wins, maybe none. Society is not reinforcing Sally's decisions even though she is, on the whole, in a much better place.
- She is in a much better place than she was decades ago when she started.
- On average, she is improving.

In scenario one, Sally is in a worse place than scenario two. However, scenario two provided little for her, her friends and her family to celebrate, whereas scenario one had hundreds of celebrations. See the disconnect?

We get greater short-term rewards for recovering from bad things than we do for avoiding them. It adds up and then compounds when others reinforce our recovery with celebration.

This is one of the paradoxical qualities of good things happening. Recognizing progress is healthy in and of itself. But we must include the consequences of bad things and the benefits of avoiding them in our mental math.

My favorite way of doing this is simple: **expand the time horizon.**

If Sally had started with a 30-year time horizon, the incentive would have been more aligned. The weight loss would have happened slower, and the longer timeline would allow her to measure a trend and test different things without urgency.

Expanding the time horizon is difficult for people. It requires forfeiting short-term wins for long-term wins: delayed gratification.

Our dopamine-addicted brains are looking for quick hits. The more expedient the win, the bigger the hit. The fastest path to emotional highs is to manufacture them:

> **Dig hole → climb out of hole → celebrate → repeat.**

Emotional high on tap.

An emotional high does not represent happiness. Let's not forget that on either side of a peak is always a valley. The more emotional highs manufactured, the more valleys manufactured. We use the "honeymoon phase" as a warning for a reason. Happiness is closing the gap between where you are now and where you want to be, and the pursuit of quick dopamine will decrease the probability of closing that gap.

The pursuit of emotional highs requires resources.

Resources are finite. With Sally, we have seen how easy it can be to sink our resources into staying in the same place by seeking short-term wins, which makes it harder to close the gap. If we can learn to appreciate when bad things don't happen, we can recapture those resources. Once recaptured, we can reallocate them to the things that actually matter. My experience has validated what people smarter than me have told me for a long time:

> *The path forward is not about more wins. Or bigger wins. It's about living the life that you want to live. To do that, we must stay out of the gutter. Avoiding bad things will take you further faster than finding more good things will.*

This is the crux of *Bumpers*. Like bumpers in a bowling alley, they keep us out of the gutter. It's a fundamental shift toward appreciating when bad things don't happen. A shift toward avoiding naive intervention. And a shift toward focusing on the things that matter most.

When your bumpers are up, you can play all-in without blowing yourself up. You can move at any speed you want. You can move at an aggressive pace or choose a pace that's slow and methodical. Resources aren't wasted digging out of holes. Every move you make is getting you closer to what matters most.

It's important to remember that everyone's

bumpers are going to look different. Some people like to travel; some people like to stay home. Parents will have different bumpers than bachelors. Quality of life is a preference-based thing. There is no right or wrong. No morality, no judgment. You don't need permission to march to the beat of your own drum, but I'm going to give it to you anyway, because...

NOBODY WINS A RACE THEY DON'T WANT TO BE IN

I've been fortunate to work with legendary athletes and business tycoons. I've spent time with thousands of entrepreneurs, some on the ascent and others going the other direction. I've learned a lot, but here is the lesson that has been most impactful for me:

People that know themselves and play by their own rules are weirdos—until they are billionaires, then they are "eccentric."

In other words, eccentric people have always had an advantage. They've always been weird. They can ignore conventional wisdom because they are clear on who they are, who they are not and what race they want to be in, and they have their bumpers up. I've also observed that:

The level of success you can *sustain* depends on how aligned your pursuits stay with your unique disposition.

There will be plenty of obstacles on your path.

There is no sense in facing them off balance. Alignment precedes balance. Balance precedes focus. Bumpers allow you to direct your focus to what matters most to you. If you have defined where you want to be and are honest about where you're at, success becomes inevitable.

Chapter 2

What Is Success?

"Success is really nothing more than the progressive realization of a worthy ideal. This means that any person who knows what they are doing and where they are going is a success. Any person with a goal towards which they are working is a successful person."

—Earl Nightingale

Think about last week.

Now think about the single day that best represents an average day for you.

- What time did you wake up?
- What did you do?
- What did you want to do but never got around to doing?
- How did you feel?

Now, take a few breaths, close your eyes and imagine your perfect day.

Imagine what it's like from the moment you wake up until the moment you go to bed and fall asleep. Not the day that society told you that you're supposed to have. Not the day that your parents or peers would judge and be proud of. The day that would be the best day for YOU.

We're building your bumpers, not theirs.

This is a simple exercise, in theory, but difficult in practice. Remember that our brains will try and convince us thinking about this is the same as doing it. It's not. It will also try to avoid defining success. It's worth fighting back. If we do not define success, we cannot know where the bumpers go.

Nobody is ever going to see your copy of *Bumpers* unless you share it with them. Since this is a "safe space" I want you to do the following exercise:

Write out your perfect day. Fight the for the details. It might take a few tries. And then finish the sentence: "I know I am successful when ________________________________."

My perfect day:

____

____

____

____

____

____.

"I know I am successful when ____."

Done? Good.

Now print it off or tear out this page. Frame it and put it somewhere you'll see it often.

This is your definition of success. From now on, weigh every decision against this picture of your future. If a decision does not get you closer to that reality, it's not closing the gap. Every step from now on is a step closer.

For example, let's pretend that part of your perfect day is:

"I am finished with work by 4 pm so I can pick up my kids from school and help with their homework."

When a giant contract lands on your desk the next day, look at your print-out before making a decision. Ask yourself:

"Does this job prevent me from being home by 4 pm every day to pick up their kids and help with their homework?"

If the answer is yes, your answer should be no.[1] Regardless of the upside, saying yes would get you further away from what you want. Remember: closer to what we want, not what will make us look successful to others.

The above is one example, but we can build bumpers in every facet of life. Simple, not easy. Our survival instinct will always convince us that "more" is the answer to everything. Fight for closer to what matters, not for more.

One of the biggest reasons we fail is not what happens to us. It's when what happens does not meet our expectations. To build bumpers, we need to get ahead of that.

---

1. *If you can't say no, it's gut check time. You lied to yourself about your perfect day. Remember, no judgment. This is designed for you to live the life you want, not the one you think are supposed to want.*

Chapter 3

Expectation Management

How do we get reality to more closely meet our expectations?

First of all, life is not a snapshot. It's a motion picture. We're programmed to think in days, weeks, months and years. Reality is not that black and white. A single frame in a movie doesn't tell us anything useful about the plot. A single snapshot in time doesn't tell us anything useful about a person's life.

We like to believe in the New Year's reset, the next month's reset or the Monday reset. Truth is, there is no reset button.

The numbers in your bank account today are a result of every decision we have made from the day you opened it until now. The amount of body fat you are carrying is a result of every decision you've made from the day you were born until now. This is not to judge your decisions or suggest that some people aren't born with advantages. It's to point out that life is a continuum and the snapshot in time is the current state of a rolling average.

As much as we want January first to be a clean slate, it's not. The reset button in our minds doesn't carry over to reality. Not even on New Year's Eve. It's important that we start to think about our life on a continuum instead of about how it looks at any single moment.

A single moment is a single point of data. Single points are dangerous.

For example, your current body weight doesn't tell me anything about your current habits. Similarly, your bloodwork is useless as a single point of data.

Here's what I mean by that: It's easy to look at someone that is overweight and think they need to change their behavior, especially if they want to lose weight. But if their weight is already trending down, changing something might be the worst thing for them. The snapshot of this moment is deceiving; it's the rolling picture that tells us what's going on.

Let's look at three separate snapshots in time and play them out together. Snapshot one is taken in early 2022. Two identical twins, John A and Billy B, get their bloodwork done and it looks like this:

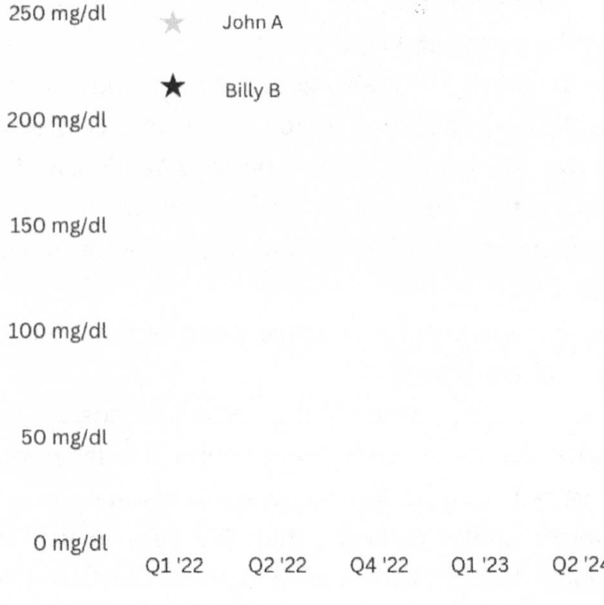

John A: 245 mg/dl
Billy B: 215 mg/dl

They rush to Google to see if they should be concerned, and the first result shows that less than 200 mg/dl is considered healthy while 200 to 239 is borderline high. At or above 240 is considered high.

Based on this snapshot, which brother's behavior needs to change the most? We may assume that John should behave more like Billy. But what if they had taken the snapshot in mid to late 2022 and it looked like this:

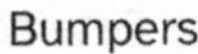

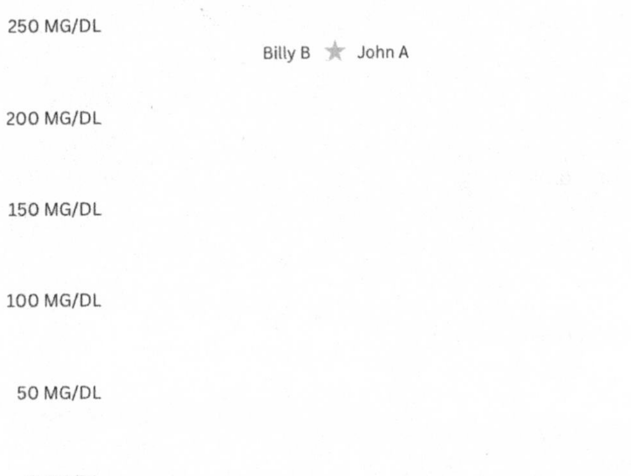

John A: 235 mg/dl
Billy B: 235 mg/dl

We might assume their current behavior is the same and they should make the same or similar changes.

If they took a snapshot in early to mid 2023 and it looked like this:

300 MG/DL
★ Billy B
★ John A
200 MG/DL
100 MG/DL
0 MG/DL
Q1 '22 Q2 '22 Q4 '22 Q1 '23 Q2 '24

John A: 265 mg/dl
Billy B: 225 mg/dl

Different story, right? Snapshot one tells us that John A is in the worse position of the two. Snapshot two tells us they were in the same position. Snapshot three tells us that John is in the better position of the two. Here's what it looks like if they took the measurement every quarter:

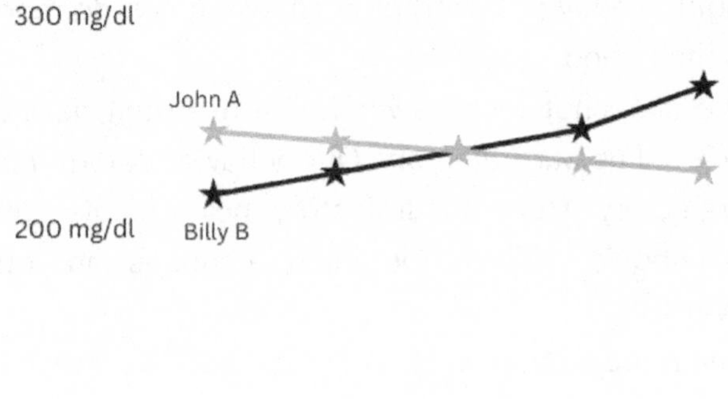

The trend suggests that John A may not need to make any changes at all. But what if he saw the initial snapshot and decided to model his behavior more after his brother, Billy? Look at Billy's trend line above.

Obviously, I am not a doctor. This is how I process data, not advice meant to be prescriptive in any way.

What I am curious about is the trend. If that health marker is trending into a healthy range, I wouldn't want to change anything. If the trend suggests the market will be in range soon, the thing to do is to let time pass.

Sometimes the best action is non-action.

Changing behavior based on a snapshot can do more harm than good.

The snapshot tells us where we are right now. It doesn't tell us our trajectory. Our behavior determines our trajectory. Thus, our trajectory, not a single data point, should inform potential changes in our behavior.

One more example:

Imagine you meet a man who has created a new algorithm for his investment fund. He tested it himself and is currently worth $50 million. Would you invest in his fund?

It depends on the trend.

Imagine these two scenarios:

Scenario 1: He started by investing $250 million into his fund and now it's worth $50 million.

Scenario 2: He started by investing $15 million into his fund and now it's worth $50 million.

Bumpers

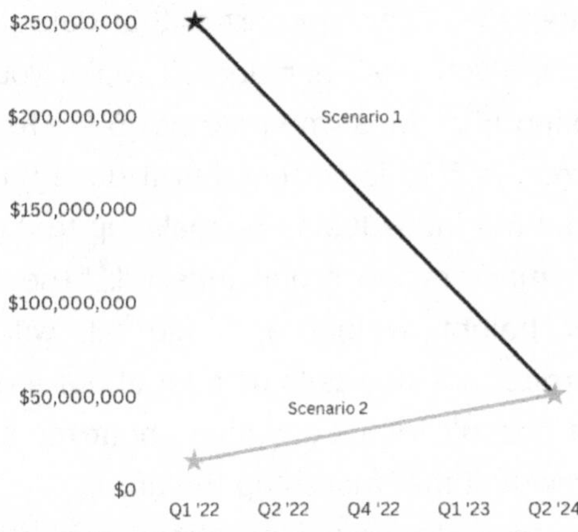

In either scenario, the snapshot is the same: he has $50 million right now. But the two scenarios tell very different stories about performance.

We want to avoid making decisions based on a single point of data. If we can get two points, we can form a line. If we can get more than two data points, we can form a trend. Whenever there are important decisions to make, I will wait until I have a trend before making it.

The frameshift from snapshots to rolling pictures also requires two other micro-frameshifts:

Micro-shift 1: From group indexing to individual indexing
Micro-shift 2: From absolute numbers to relative numbers

Group indexing is a snapshot in time of a group of people. The average American male is 5'9". If you are an American male, you are part of that data set. That doesn't make you 5'9", nor does it make you wrong for not being 5'9". Most men are not 5'9". To say the average man is 5'9" is correct, but it does not tell us much about the individuals who make up that group.

Health markers are group indexed: "The average man your height, weight and age fall within this range." Group indexing tells us a lot about a group of people. It doesn't tell us anything about the behavior of any individual that makes up the group.

I want to make decisions about myself and my behavior from data that's individually indexed to me. To index individually, we need to understand relative change.

Relative change is exactly what it sounds like.

Amazon can lose a million bucks tomorrow and it would be a relatively small loss for them. What if you lost a million bucks tomorrow?

The absolute number is the same in both cases: one million. The relative change is different. Thus, the impact is different.

A 300-pound man losing 20 pounds has lost six percent of his body weight. What if one 110-pound woman lost 20 pounds? That's 18 percent of her body weight. They both lost 20 pounds, the same absolute change. The former has likely gotten healthier, as three percent is well within a healthy range. The latter is likely in the ER.

Comparing ourselves to others in absolute terms leads to arbitrary goals with arbitrary timelines, which is juvenile at best and dangerous at worst.

Having bumpers means building for favorable, individual relative change: "Tomorrow you are going to be closer to what you want than you are today." There is no concern about where you stand compared to others today. We aren't equipped with the ability to effectively compare ourselves to others, nor do we need to.

This is the Bumpers Frameshift:

Focus less on the gap between yourself and others. Focus more on the gap between your intention and your behavior. The comparison with the most utility is the one between yourself in the past and yourself today. Focus less on absolute change and more on relative change. This is about you relative to you.

Bumpers are not designed to make you as happy as your friends pretend to be or as rich as you think your boss is. They are designed so that every decision gets you closer to what matters most to you.

Since we are managing expectations, let's get this one out of the way:

Nothing happens in a straight line.

The rolling average tells us the story that we care about.

There are no straight lines in nature. Expecting them is nonsensical and forcing them can be disastrous.

I believe that the most practical way to measure progress in the real world is the rolling average.

Complex and adaptive systems tend to be cyclic. They ebb and flow. They have peaks and valleys, ceilings and floors.

The goal is not to force a straight line by removing the cycles. It's to reduce the volatility and increase the reliability of the system. Volatility is the average distance between the ceiling and the floor. The lower the discrepancy between the two, the less volatile the system and the more control we have over the outcome.

We cannot eliminate the floor. Some days will always be a little worse than others. But we can raise it. If the ceiling stays the same but the floor rises, the rolling average improves.

Raising the floor is also efficient. Most people strive for higher highs, which is the least efficient way to make progress. By definition, your best is the best you can do. Could you maybe do better tomorrow? Sure, but the lifetime of data suggests that it will be difficult, otherwise it wouldn't be your best. Pushing yourself to do better than your best often leads to exhaustion and burnout. It's during these times of burnout we spend time on the "floor" and lower our rolling average.

In *Rigging The Game*, Dan Nicholson shares the data behind his "Highest Month Paradigm." Most companies are in their worst cash position and carry the most risk about three months *after a record month.*

Dr. Jeff Spencer has coached over 40 Olympic medalists and world champions. He has a concept called "best year, worst year." The year after their best year of performance, athletes are most likely to have their worst year.

In other words, people push so hard for a single, glorious snapshot that they tank their rolling average.

Your maximum achievability is not your maximum maintainability.

Raising the floor improves your maintainability. And it is easy: Do better than your worst.

Remember the data set that suggests it's unlikely to do better than your best? That same data suggests it's likely you can do better than your worst, and most of the time you do. But what happens if you focus on keeping the ceiling the same while raising the floor?

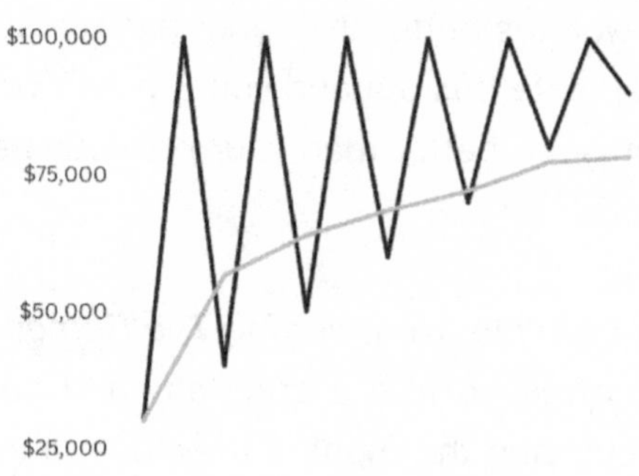

Above, you'll see the ceiling is unchanged. The "best" is never bettered. The line through the middle represents the average. In this case, it's profit per month. A few things to note:

- The average monthly revenue is growing, which means more money in the bank than the previous month. Even without a record month.
- The difference between the best months and the average is shrinking, improving reliability. Reality is becoming more likely to meet expectations.
- The difference between the worst months and the average is shrinking, improving reliability. Again, reality is becoming more likely to meet expectations.
- The worst months start to become better than the previous average. That means your new worst is better than your old average.
- Extrapolate this out and your future worst months are better than your previous best months.

Another example from *Rigging The Game*:

Dan will often go into a company and double its profits by removing the months they lose money. Just turning the negatives into zeroes doubles profits, on average. It would take a herculean effort to double profits through higher record months, as each record month increases overhead and obligation, putting future months at higher risk of being negative.

This is not to say that doing better than your best

is a bad thing. It's to say that risk-adjusted, it's not the most efficient thing to focus on. Raising the floor leads to a significant improvement in the rolling average. It requires less effort and less risk than pushing for better bests does.

A focus on raising the floor decreases the gap between your best days and your worst days. When we see this in real life, we call it consistency. In time, your floor becomes better than your ceiling ever was. Your worst day can become better than anyone else's best.

Raising the floor is not sexy. Until it is.

If you've battled weight loss, you know the struggle. If you have tried to build a business, you know the struggle. If you are a purpose-driven human with goals, you know the struggle.

Your weight is going to fluctuate every day. Your revenue numbers are going to fluctuate monthly, as are your profit margins. These are all things to measure and manage with the rolling average in mind. If we look at every snapshot as useful information...

EVERY CYCLE BECOMES A COUNTDOWN TO DOOMSDAY

Ever had a friend that checks his portfolio every hour? Or known someone that weighs themselves six times a day?

They are psychologically exhausting themselves. And it's pointless. We know that there will be peaks and valleys. We also know that a loss hurts more than an equivalent gain feels good. A high frequency of exposure can lead to incurring emotional loss, even if we are winning.

The easiest way for me to explain my thinking about complex systems is through the lens of biology. It is the most adaptive and complex of systems. It's also something that most people have all wrestled with at some point in the context of weight loss or fitness. This is the actual data from a client of a nutrition company. It's a great representation of what sustainable weight loss looks like.

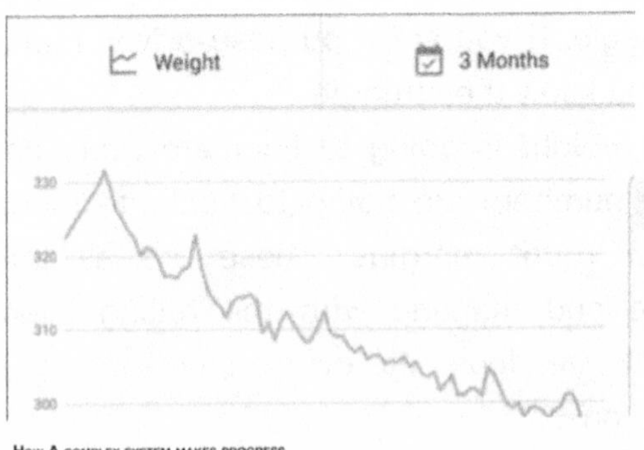

How A COMPLEX SYSTEM MAKES PROGRESS

Notice how the day-to-day progress is not a straight line. If we expected it to be, we would incur quite a bit of disappointment, which is emotional damage. Also, notice how the rolling average shows over 30 pounds lost. Since we built this with bumpers as an underpinning, it wasn't restrictive.

Thirty pounds lost over three months without restriction. That sounds like a win to me.

The graph above represents a drastic change in body composition, so drastic that it was hard for others to believe. If we picked two or three single points to gauge progress, we might've seen:

Week 1: Emotional valley. Weight gained, negative emotion incurred.
"Oh no, I've gained weight! This isn't working. I am going the wrong direction. I need to blow it all up and start over."
Week 2: Between the emotional peak and valley.
Week 3: Emotional peak.

Depending on when these arbitrary snapshots were, the data could suggest no progress. It could lead us to throw up our hands, play victim and quit a perfect effectively strategy. This is the risk of single data points.

Here is what works for me:

Optimize by taking frequent enough measurements to get a rolling average. Ignore the day-to-day fluctuation and track the average over time. It's more effective and WAY less of a cognitive load to carry around. Like the graph above, there will be peaks and valleys. The goal is not more wins. It's that every peak is the same or a little higher than the previous peaks and each valley a little higher than the previous valley.

I've seen many ambitious people attempt to straight-line a complex system. Every single one of them has blown themselves up and had to start over. *They didn't know how to appreciate when bad things didn't happen.*

But that's not the only reason to collect and track data over a long period of time.

Chapter 4
The Illusion of Learning

I fancy myself a student. I like to learn. I am an entrepreneur and, sometimes, a visionary. This has long been considered a recipe for success by the Silicon Valley "fail and fail fast" type. I disagree.

I don't think it's entirely false, just incomplete.

People with my disposition try to learn by trying, failing and doing so quickly. It sounds good, but it creates a hidden long-tail risk. The short-term, immediately observable consequences have taught us something, but not everything. The mistake we make is thinking that we have learned completely from experience. This "touch the stove" method of learning has a dark side.

Learning through doing helps us understand the "detail complexity." We figure things out, measure the consequences and then make a decision. Is this thing we figured out a viable solution or is it something we should continue to work on? The thought process is pragmatic enough for us to accept it as complete.

The problem is this:

By closing the loop and deciding we have learned a thing completely, we miss the "dynamic complexities." The consequences of our actions appear somewhere else in space and time, and we fail to recognize their cause. For example:

- A huge 10-year deal you closed was cause for celebration, but it also put a tremendous amount of stress on the accounting department. The way you closed the deal created issues that only pop up during tax season, five years down the road. The accounting team gets blamed for being late, even though the way you closed the deal years earlier is the root of the problem.
- A work vacation you take every year makes your spouse or your family question your motives. After three years, it shows up as a relationship-shaking argument about something that seems completely unrelated.
- Your 18-year-old daughter has developed disordered eating patterns and it breaks your heart, so you wage war on magazines, television and social media for giving her an unrealistic image of beauty—without considering how your own body dysmorphia as a suspected influence, or the extreme crash dieting she watched you do when she was eight years old.

These are dynamic consequences—you know, the consequences we don't think about and are not immediately obvious. The things that come back full circle and kick us in the ass. Their delay is so long that we can't track events back to the initial behavior that caused them. By the time they happen, the effect seems so divorced from the real cause that we attribute it to the wrong thing, learn the wrong thing and wage war against imaginary enemies.

In other words: we blame others for our mistakes.

When this happens, there is no learning happening. If there is no learning, nothing is improving. Instead, we launch crusades against everything and everyone else.

Here's a very real personal example:

Seven months into working with a new company, we eclipsed $100,000 a month. No paid advertising, no website or anything. That's not to say we didn't work hard or that it was easy—it's just the way it happened.

The growth was as unexpected as it was exciting.

Lost in the excitement, we made a few changes. We swapped our process-based goals for outcome-based goals. Instead of measuring our behavior every day and allowing revenue to be a byproduct of it, we measured revenue every day.

We started focusing on numbers and timelines. Goals based on speculation, not our actual behavior. (In other words, we set arbitrary goals and timelines.)

Up to this point, my team and I had only three criteria:

1. We work with MKP (My Kinda People) only.
2. No headaches. This was a side business we set up to spend time with people we liked to spend time with.
3. No two people doing the same thing. I wanted diversity and safety, and most people are more open when their competitors are not in the room.

These were our original bumpers for the business.

Anyway, back to the revenue goal...

Over the next two months, we had a series of failed advertising campaigns. We also saw increased churn and much lower levels of enjoyment for what we were doing. It seemed like a perfect storm: employees were making mistakes, our clients were struggling and Facebook kept changing its algorithm.

It was easy to blame everything and everyone else (dynamic complexity at work).

But here's the truth. It's not easy to write this, but, it's necessary to share with you:

We violated our bumpers, and it was 100 percent on me.

We made a series of bad decisions that looked like great decisions at the time. Our revenue was skyrocketing reinforcing that I was learning something. I wasn't learning what I thought I was learning, and was falling into the illusion of learning instead.

We optimized for the wrong thing because of short-term, repeat dopamine hits. Without bumpers to fall back on and check ourselves, I would still be blaming others.

So, the first-order consequence was as follows:

I learned that if I advertised a certain way in the short-term, our revenue increased dramatically. That was not incorrect; it was incomplete. The problem is most people would stop learning right there.

Marketers, parents, teachers and many others are spinning their wheels looking for answers in the wrong places. As complexities become more dynamic with time, they increase their effort—and that effort goes into pulling the wrong levers. They end up creating more problems for themselves without realizing it.

Without an initial set of bumpers, there is no obvious way to step out of the hamster wheel.

How often are you pointing fingers at others for things stemming from a decision you made in the past? How much of your own misfortune are you creating without being aware of it?

It's a difficult question to face.

But if you're still in the game, let's build some bumpers to answer it.

Chapter 5

Building Bumpers

To restate the obvious:

The gutters determine where the bumpers go.

The first step in raising the floor is avoiding bad things and staying out of the gutter. To determine where to build our bumpers, we need to know what to avoid.

You don't need to list every bad thing you can imagine, but there are likely a few things you refuse to accept in life. Start there.

I have found that each person has a handful of traps they are prone to. They are unique to the individual. Some are people pleasers; others rotate too far the other way out of stubbornness. Some are too trusting; others are too closed off.

The key here is to identify the traps that you are the most prone to falling into. Those are your gutters. Once you identify them, turn them into commandments for yourself: the things you need to protect against.

I call them non-negotiables.

DETERMINE THE NON-NEGOTIABLES OF YOUR LIFE

When I ask someone what they want their life to look like, they start telling me about how much money they want to make. Without fail, they roll right into revenue or income goals.

It's not that I don't care how much your business generates, as that's part of the equation. But that is not the question I asked. In this case, I asked what you want your *life* to look like.

You should already have a picture of this for yourself from earlier. Using that image of success, write down a few non-negotiables.

One trick I find helpful is to imagine your future self living your perfect day, then list the things you will *not* be doing in that life. What are the things you know you would no longer be doing in your dream life? If future you living that perfect life wouldn't be arguing about politics on Facebook, then stop arguing about politics on Facebook.

This can be a helpful guide to prevent self-sabotage. What are the things that are most likely to knock you off course?

For example, maybe:

- You refuse to miss your son's baseball games.
- You refuse to be at the office after 5 pm.
- You never want to be too busy to take your wife or husband on vacation (I see you, badass business ladies).

Take a moment to write down your non-negotiables that can act as your keystone bumpers. Remember: these are **non-negotiables.** Not "it would be nice if" criteria but things you **absolutely REFUSE to negotiate** so your life can be what you want it to be.

This is a list of single decisions that make a thousand other decisions for you later on. Making one decision that makes thousands of decisions for you later is powerful.

Here is my list at the time of writing this:

From now on, I refuse to:

1. Negotiate with myself.
2. Start something new that I am not willing to do forever.
3. Judge people or try to win arguments.
4. Accept my way as the only possible or the best way.

I'm going to break mine down for you below, but I'm not suggesting that you adopt any of them. I'll only share the thought process behind each one.

But first, make your own list:

From now on, I refuse to:

1. ______________________________
2. ______________________________
3. ______________________________
4. ______________________________
5. ______________________________
6. ______________________________
7. ______________________________
8. ______________________________

Now, here is the thought process behind my non-negotiables:

1. "I refuse to negotiate with myself."

This is one of two rules that I stick to most steadfastly, and here's why:

If I know for a 100 percent fact that I am committed to never negotiating with myself, I am going to stop making stupid deals with myself. This is not about being more rigid in action, *it's about being more intentional about what I decide to do.*

Remember the gap? Much of the gap comes from making deals with yourself you don't intend to follow through on. I commit to fewer things for myself to keep a tight gap.

It's that simple.

When I put something in my calendar or when I commit to something, I am 100 percent committed and married to it—and because I have made this a non-negotiable, I have to be mindful about what I say I will do.

If you give yourself an inch, you will let yourself take a mile.

Committing to this rule forces me to create the calendar that I want, the one that will make me happy instead of the one I wish I wanted or I think I "should" want. The calendar of tyranny that most of us create for ourselves leads to us rebelling against it anyway. Humans will always rebel against tyranny—even if the tyrant is oneself.

Ultimately, bumpers don't exist to protect us from the outside world. They protect us from ourselves.

Refusing to negotiate with myself helps me stick to my second rule, which is...

2. "I refuse to start something I am not willing to do forever."

This one always catches people off guard, because they think it means I have to do everything I do forever. That's not the point. Let me use a short thought experiment to explain:

Let's pretend for a moment that you want to lose 30 pounds.

To lose that weight, you decide to cut all carbohydrates and exercise twice a day, seven days a week. Now, let's say that while starving yourself and exercising two times a day, you do, indeed, lose the weight. To keep that weight off, you have married yourself to starving and over-exercising.

Worse, what happens if you sprain an ankle and you can't exercise for three weeks? It's not going to be pretty, because you have achieved the outcome by means that are not sustainable.

Any time you reach a goal with a method you are not willing to use forever, the progress you make is fragile. You have a thing, and you got the thing in a way that you're not willing or able to keep doing.

This leaves two options:

1. Do something you don't want to do forever.
2. Lose the thing you worked so hard for.

I know that if I'm not willing to do something forever, the results won't be sustainable. Of course, I will still do all kinds of things I may not want to do forever—but only if I'm okay with the results not being sustainable.

If it's truly important to me, I won't start anything unless my 900-day progress is going to be better than my 90-day progress.

This is true in business, and this is true in relationships.

If you plan on being around beyond the next 90 days, then it would behoove you to stop thinking, *Can*

I do this for the next 90 days? Instead, start asking yourself, *Is this something I am willing to do forever?*

If not, step back and explore some other more sustainable options. Again, this is not to say that you shouldn't embark on your journey—only that your non-negotiables act as a forcing function to find a sustainable way to reach them.

"Am I willing to do this forever?"

That question will change your life. And if you don't agree with me, that's okay, because...

3. "I refuse to judge people or try to win arguments."

Nothing inhibits productivity more than wasting time and energy. Both are valuable and both are finite. Nothing wastes more time and energy than judging others, taking a position against them and spending time and energy on defending it so you can be right.

It is not profitable. It is not productive. It is not required for your happiness.

It requires a lot of intellectual security to be okay with being wrong, but it's so powerful to live in that place. Proving other people wrong does not move me closer to my goals.

I had a realization years ago, and it's going to trigger some people:

People pay me a lot of money to judge them, so I'm not going to do it for free.

I mean, if people pay for space in your brain, why give it to others at no charge? Next time someone tries to occupy space in your brain at no charge to them, think about what you are telling the universe about what you're worth.

How liberating is that?

I know how that can sound, and I would never say it out loud to somebody else. But it's such a useful tool that I would be remiss not to share it with you.

Someone in your life is *earning* space in your brain. They may pay for it with money, time, attention, love, care or whatever it is. Don't disrespect them by giving space away to others for free.

Write down your non-negotiables and think about what they mean to you. After that, move on to building those bumpers in five steps:

1. **The Science of Hindsight**: Seeing things for what they are, turning theory into application and creating something we can solve for.
2. **Patterns and Consistency**: Strategically raising the floor.
3. **Eliminating Decision Fatigue**: Raising the floor on autopilot.
4. **Novelty**: Having some effin' fun without derailing your progress.

5. **Suffocating Guilt and Shame**: The simple truth that there is no place in your best life for these emotions.

And I will walk you through each one.

Chapter 6

The Science of Hindsight

Alright, here it is:

If you want to do something extraordinary, you can't do what ordinary people do.

You're going to have to look where ordinary people won't look: in the mirror.

If you've made it this far, you're up for the task.

The first step of this process is to compile your current day-to-day activity, because even the most detailed map in the world is useless without the little "you are here" sticker. To build anything useful, we must get clear on our current position.

There are two ways to do this.

1. You can look at last week's calendar and log what you did every single day. I prefer 30-minute blocks, but do the best you can.

Or:

2. You can track your next week. Write down and record, in 30-minute increments, everything you do from the time you wake up to the time you go to sleep. Try not to leave any minute unaccounted for. Do your best not to change your behavior just because you are tracking it.

Generally, the first method is more effective. When we are cognizant of the fact that we are tracking our behavior, we adjust a little bit to meet our biases. Said another way: we change our behavior when we know it is being tracked.

We want the clearest vision of our average behavior. It is the science of seeing things clearly, which I call **the Science of Hindsight**.

If you can't go back a week, do your best over the next week to track your time, behavior and patterns.

It might look like this:

	Work	Social Media	Family Time	Eating	Sleeping
Monday	5	6	3.5	3.5	6
Tuesday	6	5	4.5	4.5	4
Wednesday	6	7	3	5	3
Thursday	9	4	3	2	6
Friday	7	6	3	4	4
Saturday	12	2	0	2	8
Sunday	3	7	2	5	7
Total	48	37	19	26	38

Now, these are arbitrary numbers that represent hours in the day. Your day may have more buckets and will look a little bit different, but do your best to *be as accurate as possible with how you're actually spending your time.*

It feels overwhelming at times, but we will simplify it. You can start with the super broad strokes and narrow it down over time. Remember: relative change. For example, you could start with three buckets: work, home and sleep, and then add new ones as you discover them. Start where you are.

Another way to say it is this: zero to one is an infinite range of relative change, so simply completing this exercise alone will lead to positive changes.

Remember: the doer is always less handicapped than the thinker. You don't have to do this exercise to completion this week. You just have to have more of it done than you did yesterday. See how this works?

Now, stop reading and come back when the task is done.

Okay, got it?

Good. Here is what we do next:

Take the total number of hours from each bucket and list them out like this:

- **Work**: 48 hours a week
- **Social Media**: 37 hours a week
- **Family Time**: 19 hours a week
- **Time Spent Eating**: 26 hours a week
- **Sleep**: 38: hours a week

When compiled like this, the data can be alarming. But this is an important step, and it is important that we do not make any drastic changes.

Reality is reality. And the best place to start is always right where you are. Anywhere else will only hurt your progress.

I'm going to show you how to build bumpers without any major lifestyle changes so that they are sustainable. You will learn which levers to pull and when to pull them.

Once we have the data, we will turn it into sustainable, repeatable patterns. This will help reduce system volatility and raise the floor.

PATTERNS AND CONSISTENCY

Now, we strategically raise the floor for long-term success.

We tend to do more on the days we feel good and less on the days we feel crummy. Both lead to compensation. We try to make up for bad days by increasing output on the other days, or we take a day off after an exceptional day of output.

But this increases volatility and breaks feedback loops.

When Jim Collins set out to find out why companies thrive when others do not, he discovered the concept of The 20-Mile March.

The 20-Mile March is a concept about consistency: identifying the gap and timeline, averaging things out and consistently performing at the average.

It says that it's not the 10x-ers pushing for growth who keep winning. The repeat performers are the companies that plan and optimize for consistency.

Here's the key to the 20-Mile March: *On days you feel like you can do more, don't.*

Instead, hold back to conserve energy. On days you *don't* feel well, all you have to do is reach the marker. Some days you push, some days you hold back. But you never blow yourself up or fall behind.

On the days you feel crummy, you do XYZ because it's required.

On the days you feel great, you *still* do XYZ—because if you do too much, the next floor might be lower than the previous one. Do not add more on the "good" days unless you can commit to doing more on the "crummy" days as well.

Please understand: *The rolling average does not increase if raising the ceiling also lowers the floor.*

As long as you still have crummy days, focus on making those better. It will improve the average more than improving the good days. We aren't being less ambitious. We're reallocating resources to what will move the needle the most.

Here is how to do that:

First, determine the things you're going to do every day.

From the example above, let's assume the things we know we are going to do consistently are:

- Work six days a week.
- Be on social media every day.

- Have family time every day.
- Eat every day.
- Sleep every night.

Then, we do the math to average it out:

- **Work**: 48 hours a week/6 days a week = 8 hours a day
- **Social Media**: 37 hours a week/ 7 days a week = 5.2 hours a day
- **Family Time**: 19 hours a week/ 7 days a week = 2.7 hours a day
- **Time Spent Eating**: 26 hours a week/ 7 days a week = 3.7 hours a day
- **Sleep**: 38 hours a week/7 days a week = 5.5 hours a day

In this case, you could very well take the .2 away from social media out of the family time and get nice round numbers. That's what I would do, anyway.

Your breakdown may look different if you work more or fewer days of the week, but I think you get the concept. We're just trying to get a rolling average that can inform us of the efficacy of our behavior over time.

Here is what you do next:

Put it on your calendar. Yep, exactly as it averages out.

You're going to want to change it a little bit. Don't.

Even though you may not actually do the same thing every day, seeing this stuff averaged out will give you a baseline. This is the rolling average we will measure from in the future, which will allow you to make micro-adjustments moving forward. It is your personal 20-Mile March.

This is what I have found to be the easiest way to build this:

- Plug in your sleep hours.
- Plug in your work hours.
- Then, plug in your eating hours.

For productivity and biological reasons, I try to do these three things at the same time every day. If you are a shift worker or have a fluctuating schedule, plug in the important things that change the least from week to week.

- Next, plug in your family time.
- You can leave your social media time white or enter it in and schedule it. I'm hoping that you find better stuff to do with that time but for now, start where you're at!

This is what my day looks like at the time of writing:

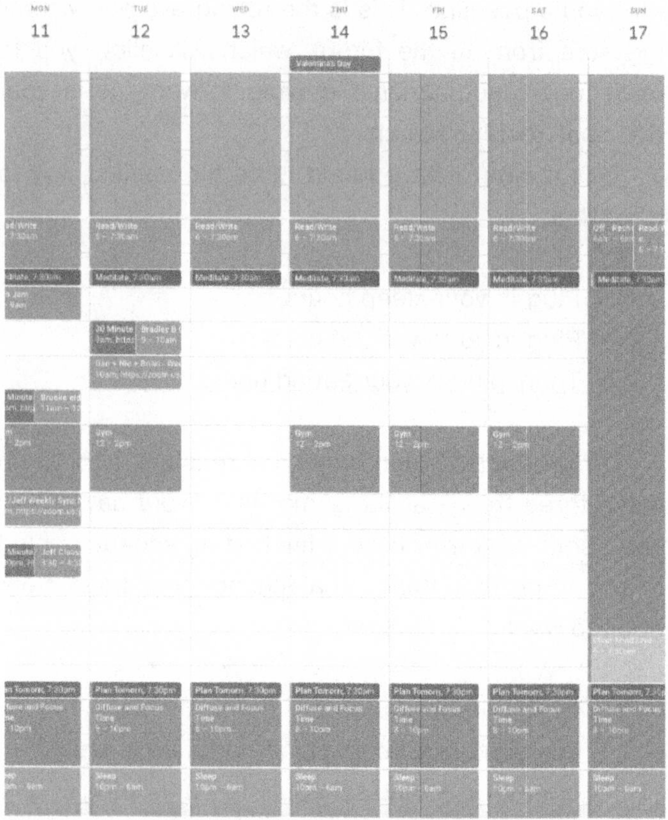

As you can see by the white space, I have a ton of time here and there to do whatever I want. But it didn't start that way. It started exactly how I am telling you to do it right now.

So, get this into your calendar to match your real-world schedule the best you can, and I would take a screenshot for your own records. Months from now, you can do this exercise again and see the space you have made for yourself.

Chapter 7

Eliminating Decision Fatigue

Now, we learn how to raise the floor on autopilot.

Look at my calendar again and notice that I do the same thing at the same time every day.

In terms of productivity, this eliminates all unnecessary and redundant decision-making. They're habits. They are set on autopilot and they get done every day without any mental energy. This means that I'm making progress every single day on autopilot.

Take a moment to play with your calendar and determine how many things you can put on autopilot. This will help you develop habits that will carry you closer to your goals. There are some tricks to making new stuff stick, but this should be pretty straightforward.

If you need help with habit formation, I strong recommend *Tiny Habits* by BJ Fogg. BJ is the founder of Stanford Behavior Design Lab, and his book is the most practical I've seen on habits.

This is probably the most important thing when it comes to my personal productivity:

Even if I do nothing new today, I will have read for a few hours, written for a few hours, gone to the gym and eaten the same amount of food.

The things I have on autopilot are more than most people will ever get done through herculean effort, and it's not because I am more talented or work harder. It's because I took the time to build bumpers.

Remember the whole drinking a gallon of water only 71 percent of the time thing? It's not sexy, but until you are *consistently* doing what you plan on doing, the next step is to get a little closer to doing it next week. The plan is not changing, but your floor will be rising.

Once your behavior matches the plan, make a tiny tweak to your bumpers calendar. Your brain will try and convince you that a larger tweak is better, but you know better now, right? Keep the gap small.

Small change → Work on behavior until it matches the new plan → another small change.

This keeps the gaps to a minimum and the floor rising.

It takes time, but time is undefeatable. It's going to pass anyway. Without bumpers, time is your worst enemy. When you do you have them, it becomes your best friend and the ultimate advantage.

Chapter 8

Novelty

In all this structure, it's important to learn how to have some effin' fun without derailing your progress.

When you're just getting started, I would adjust your bumpers weekly or biweekly at most—and even then only slightly.

This means that once they are set, as long as the scheduled stuff gets done, you are moving forward. Everything else is novelty: have fun, take a nap, hang with your family or take on a side project (within your bumpers)! For full disclosure, I wrote this book in the white spaces of my calendar.

If the scheduled stuff does not get done, you have two options:

1. **Work on getting your behavior to match the plan.** In this case, the plan stays the same, but the behavior changes. Do not feel guilt or shame about it, just find out

why you're not doing the things you planned on doing.

2. **Adjust the plan to more closely match your behavior.** In this case, the plan changes to match behavior. This also closes the gap, which gives us a tighter feedback loop. We cannot gauge the efficacy of the plan until our behavior is aligned with it.

This is an adjustment using the Science of Hindsight—you know, stuff that actually happened in real life. Every week you can make a tiny adjustment, either narrowing down or opening up your bumpers. But since it's a conscious decision, you are now steering the ship. You also have a tighter grip on the cause and effect.

For example, you could add an hour of sleep, which cuts into an hour of social media, and then ride that out for a week. If you're successful, you can make another tiny change. If not, try again.

At the risk of being repetitive:

To get results, your plan does not have to change. Your behavior does.

So, adjust your behavior a little bit and let time pass. Spend the rest of your free time doing things that make you happy. As long as you are adjusting your bumpers consistently, you are making progress.

It's counterintuitive, but if you are honest about

where you're at and focus on consistency, you'll have way more free time than you can imagine. You'll be able to make more progress with less rigidity than you ever thought possible.

And then, something else magical happens: **guilt and shame disappear.**

Chapter 9

Suffocating Guilt and Shame

By now, you may already see that in your best life, there is no place for guilt and shame—but if not, I'll illustrate.

It's the wildest thing that people feel guilt from not working enough, not making enough or whatever.

Without bumpers, it's easy to develop the idea that we must suffer to deserve anything worthwhile. That's human logic for you: to be happy, we must be miserable. Our brains get stuck on this idea, and our behavior suggests that we believe it.

To be happy, I must be miserable. What a paradox.

The reality is if you set your bumpers, your brain will immediately start to adjust. As long as you're inside the bumpers, you're groovy. You're moving toward what you want, you deserve it and guilt and shame start to disappear.

The marketing efforts of others will continue to try and widen your gaps by creating desires, telling you all the things you should do or have. That's okay. If they fit within your bumpers, great. If not, let them go.

Years ago, Dr. Kashey wrote my team and I the following blurb for an old website describing the impact that bumpers had on his life (though I've swapped out some language for the sake of context):

> *Life in the 21st century is a double-edged sword. What we've gained in breadth, we've lost in depth.*
>
> *The great irony of the information age is that we have more knowledge than ever but increasingly less of an idea what to do with it.*
>
> *Wrapped in shiny paper and large words, dogmatism abounds in the world, leaving individuals less confident that they're closer to the answer than before.*
>
> *Bumpers.*
>
> *It's not about laziness, greed or gluttony. It is about having the ability to recognize that the war is usually a civil one, wherein the only path to progress is to make peace with ourselves.*
>
> *Having bumpers means being flexible.*
>
> *We know that well-being can be achieved from many approaches.*

Only in recognizing our own needs can we be in a position to prioritize what we hold most dear.

When we hashtag #bumpers, we do so to remind people they have the freedom to choose; to provide themselves with opportunity.

You can't say no if you don't even have the chance to say yes.

Variety is the spice of life, and having bumpers means giving yourself permission to choose what is right for you.

Continuously strive to find ways to improve the quality of your life.

Choose joy and security over guilt and shame.

Read that last line again. And again.

Bumpers allow you to do the things you want to do, and to choose to feel joy and security instead of guilt and shame.

To recap, the process of building bumpers has five steps:

1. **The Science of Hindsight**: Seeing things for what they are, turning theory into

application and creating something we can solve for.

2. **Patterns and Consistency**: Strategically raising the floor.
3. **Eliminating Decision Fatigue**: Raising the floor on autopilot.
4. **Novelty**: Having some effin' fun without derailing your progress.
5. **Suffocating Guilt and Shame**: The simple truth that there is no place in your best life for these emotions.

If it seems overly simplistic, that's because it is.

If I were smarter, I would have been able to make it even simpler. But the reality is that most people are pushing harder and harder on the gas with the other foot on the brakes.

The most efficient path forward is often the simplest one:

Learn to appreciate when bad things don't happen.

It is time to bridge the chasm. To close the gap between what you know you should be doing and the things you are actually doing.

As simple as it is, there will be a few pitfalls. And since you now appreciate when bad things don't happen, I want to warn you to keep an eye out for them.

Chapter 10
Pitfalls

"Our emotions and cognitions are so vivid, so comfortable, so perfectly catered to us, it is no wonder that we so confidently rely on them in formulating our own behavior and in perceiving the behavior of others. Yet, with our eyes half-closed, with every step we take away from the real world into our imaginations, we create a reality that is more and more idiosyncratic and, in so doing, we widen the communication gap between ourselves and others."

—Elizabeth Louise Newton

One of the texts I keep at my desk at all times is called *The Rocky Road From Actions to Intentions*. It's a dissertation written by Elizabeth Louise Newton, a doctoral student at Stanford in 1990.

Newton recruited 80 Stanford graduate students, gave them a list of 25 popular songs and asked them to tap three tunes with their finger. The subjects were then asked to estimate what percentage of the audience would be able to name the tune they were tapping.

The subjects guessed that, on average, the audience would be able to guess the tune 50 percent of the time. The guesses ranges from 10 percent to 95 percent. In reality, the audience was able to guess the tune 2.5 percent of the time—a rate that was entirely outside the range of estimates.

Not only had all these Stanford graduate students overestimated their ability to communicate what was in their head; they grossly overestimated it.

In the second study, Newton had them tap the tune and observe the listener as it was being tapped. Now that the tapper had tapped the tune and seen the response from the listener, what did they feel the probability was that the listener understood the tune? 50 percent again. Reality? The listener was able to guess the tune 3 percent of the time.

Not only do we grossly overestimate our ability to communicate to others, but we also grossly overestimate how well we have communicated after the communication has taken place.

This is, by and large, because when the tappers are tapping, they have the accompaniment in their head to fill in the gaps and they assume the listener is hearing some of what they are hearing.

The Rocky Road From Actions to Intentions highlights the first pitfall: communication.

More accurately, the illusion of communication taking place.

When you change your behavior, it will concern the people in your life. This is especially true for your loved ones: your wife, your husband, your kids and your best friend(s). This is going to be frustrating for you. You are finally doing something for yourself and it will feel as if everyone is working against you. It will be easy to get mad at them or think about quitting.

Slow your roll, homie.

These people care about you.

They should express concern about drastic behavior change. Someone acting differently overnight is concerning.

Chances are, they aren't mind readers. They do not know that you read this book. They have no idea why your behavior has changed. You know you are doing something positive and why you are doing it. You have the accompaniment; they don't. If you expect everyone else in your life to be able to read your mind, you are creating your own suffering.

If you are going to make a change, even for the better, do not assume that others will understand it—not until you take the time to help them understand. It's your responsibility to articulate to them what is happening and why it is important to you (or you can buy them a crystal ball for Christmas).

Communication isn't easy. As we see in *The Rocky Road*, the biggest problem with it is the illusion that it has taken place. Aside from self-sabotage, the biggest barrier to success is friction from others, but it is *not* because they don't want you to succeed. They do. They just don't understand what is going on or why. For all they know, you're having an affair or started using drugs or something.

Be an adult. Have a conversation.

The second thing to be aware of is the danger of arbitrary goals and arbitrary timelines.

I touched on them a bit before, but I want to circle back here.

The story I told earlier about chasing revenue goals and going into a mini-spiral is an example. We may want to achieve X goal by Y date, but staring at the finish line is not going to bring it any closer any faster.

The process is the shortcut.

The best thing any of us can do is to focus on the process and judge ourselves only on our behavior for that particular day. You make money by getting better at things that make money, not by staring at your bank account all day.

You can't win the game if you're staring at the scoreboard the entire time. You don't get to choose if the bases are loaded when you come up to bat. The only thing you have control over is your behavior and your preparedness. It's going to make you better or worse tomorrow.

Bumpers give you the highest probability of being in the best position possible when the opportunity comes. Each arbitrary goal and timeline will only drive down your ability to get the things you want most in life.

You have bumpers now. This is just a start, but it will have more of a profound impact on your life than you could ever imagine.

Get to work.

—Nic

Final Thoughts and Other Good Stuff

I have a deep appreciation and a tremendous amount of gratitude for you. If you're here, you made it to the end. I hope you are able to apply something from *Bumpers* that will have a positive impact on your life. I know there are many things you could have done with your time, so I'm grateful you spent it here reading this.

Other stuff you might enjoy if you found value in *Bumpers*:

(Note: Every non-fiction writer or thinker ought to include a section like this one. Why? Well, if you made it this far, odds are that your worldview includes a bias in favor of the content of this book. So here are other things you may enjoy.)

Bumpers Checklist, Workbook and Audio Companion:

FreeBumpersBook.com

Here you can download the workbook designed to help keep track of relative change. The audio companion is not me reading the book; it's a presentation I did for Joe Polish's Genius Network. It explores the practical applications of *Bumpers* and goes deeper into some of the concepts from the book.

Twitter:

Twitter.com/peternicson

I use Twitter as my notepad. It's basically a look into my thoughts day to day.

Force Multipliers:

subscribe.nicpeterson.com

This is an AI newsletter designed for me as a reader. It finds the most interesting stuff on the internet, curates it for me and then optimizes based on my engagement. Peter Diamandis's AI company built it for me and it's my favorite email to get each week. If you are interested in what I am reading, sign up. It's free.

***Rigging The Game* by Dan Nicholson:**

RiggingAmazon.com

Dan Nicholson is a wealth wizard. He and I spend a lot of time together, so you will find similarities in our frameworks. He has a much more refined delivery than I do, which some people prefer.